An auntie and two cousins appear. What a surprise! Their presence changed everything for me. I had longed for this for a long time and now, it became real. This made my usual happy summertime even more delightful. There was fun! I mean fun. My story will became even more interesting as you read on.

Pearl Drops in My Summer

Natalie Nwanekwu

iUniverse LLC
Bloomington

Pearl Drops in My Summer

iUniverse books may be ordered through booksellers or by contacting:

iUniverse LLC
1663 Liberty Drive
Bloomington, IN 47403
www.iuniverse.com
1-800-Authors (1-800-288-4677)

ISBN: 978-1-4917-3402-5 (sc)
ISBN: 978-1-4917-3401-8 (e)

Library of Congress Control Number: 2014908623

Printed in the United States of America.

iUniverse rev. date: 05/15/2014

Names, and some details of this book were changed to protect privacy of the concerned persons

About the Author

Natalie Nwanekwu the author wrote this book when she was 11 years which is mostly a combination of her journal entries. Her outstanding academic performance is highly impressive. Nathalie has never had a grade lower that 'A' since her first grade in school till present (8th grade). This is quite evident from the numerous distinguished academic awards she received beginning in 2nd grade. Natalie is an avid reader. Prominently hanging in her room is a '100 Books' certificate of award which she accomplished during her 2nd grade, conferred on her on the 7th of March, 2008. Still up till now, she maintains her scholarly excellence with series of awards. She received the 6th and 8th grade English Language Arts awards. Some of the other received awards are; Meaningful economics Composition, nomination for the District Science Fair, National Reading and DCAS. Nathalie's exceptional brilliance is so widespread that her academic performance is not exclusive to any subject area. Though in grade 8, she is pursuing a 10th grade level math and is contemplating pursuing a grade 11th since she has gotten too comfortable with a grade 10th math. Towards this ability, she also received the Forum to Advance minorities in Engineering award (FAME).

Natalie is passionate about reading and writing. She reads at an average of two books per month. She is highly thrilled that she could carefully and intelligently piece together a segment of her life in writing for the public audience.

Dedication

To my parents for being the reason for all that I represent.

Acknowledgement

A special thanks to Dr. Odilia Osakwe for her outpouring of love and care that strengthened me throughout the writing process, making sure that my journal entries were up to date. Her support and encouragement helped bring this vision to completion.

To my friends, cousins and the rest of the members of my extended family, you are the heart of this story.

Contents

About the Author vii

Dedication.. ix

Acknowledgement... xi

Preface xv

August 9, 2011

    The Arrival..1

August 10, 2011

    The Great Cousins-Maurine and I.................. 3

August 11, 2011

    The Airplane Experience............................... 6

August 12, 2014

    The Outing.. 8

August 13, 2011

    The Chewing Gum 14

August 14, 2011

    The Special Touch...18

August 15, 2011

    Unexpected Displacement............................ 26

August 16, 2011

    The Sock War.. 33

August 17, 2011

    The-Sprinkler—over

    -Trampoline Idea 41

August 18, 2011

    Trampoline for Sam..................................... 46

August 19, 2011

    Questions about Heaven.............................. 52

August 20, 2011

    Evie's Birthday.. 56

August 21, 2011

    The Swimming Pool Miracle 64

August 23, 2011

    The Earthquake... 67

August 24, 2011

    Travelling Home 73

Preface

This piece of writing was the work of a very young girl named Nathalie who lives with her parents and two brothers in the city Newark, Delaware. It narrates a journal entry of all the events that took place during a summer vacation with her aunty and cousins in her family home residence. Her cousins and their parents live in Brooklyn, New York and her auntie lives in Toronto, Ontario, Canada.

Traditionally, the cousins often make frequent visits to her home during the special holidays which would be the Thanksgiving or Christmas. But this lasted mostly for the weekend. These days of the year are always anticipated and always marked by extensive preparations, meditations and passionate feelings for these special 'D-days'. Once they arrive, her joys escalate but even though, end very quickly as they depart in two days' time.

Natalie's aunt had a 3-week vacation time to spend in her house and then thought it wise to bring along two of her cousins from New York. One of the cousins, Maurine is her closest tie as they were born about 3-weeks apart in the same apartment before their mothers eventually separated. Amidst the separation, their tie remained as very close till present.

Usually, Natalie's summertime would be spent traveling to places but the 2011 summer was spent in her house and differently. This time, there were several activities in the home that kept the candle of joy glowing throughout. Her father travelled for vacation and was not present at the time. In the mornings, Natalie's mother would go to work leaving her in the company of her aunt, siblings and cousins. Natalie would not think of any other vacation better than the seemingly unending days filled with fun activities amidst her family and family guests. This work was presented in a chronological order starting from guest arrival, August 9 to day of travelling home August 24. The happy moments started from August 9 up till the morning of August 23. This period of time was filled with lessons, spiritual activities, reflections, recapitulations, outings, gaming and sporting activities draped with sporadic and riveting jokes; and laughing moments.

Towards the end of this vacation period, as the time for Natalie's family guests' departure approached, on August 23, 2011, at 1:51 pm EDT, an unexpected earthquake touched the ground and fell pictures hanging on the wall in the house. It was the magnitude 5.8 Virginia earthquake reported as the largest to have occurred in the U.S. east of the Rocky Mountains since 1897. It rocked several of the U.S. states and Canadian provinces and was felt by more people than any other earthquake in the U.S. history. The pangs were felt and dealt with in the arms of one another.

Subsequent to the aftershock ripples was a newsline report announcing an ensuing hurricane Irene expected to travel along the Caribbean and East Coast of the United States. As at the time of the announcement, it was still moving and had already affected some of the US east-bound states leaving a tremendous damage of life and property on its track. The news appeared so abrupt because, the children had engaged all the televisions in the house to games and children favorites. Adults in the house were caught up in these children's 'funfair' and did not listen to the news as well. It was not expected to reach the Newark city. Thus, family guests left in good faith.

Suddenly, following the guests departure, a sardonic twist of tragedy began to force its way through her graced doorways when the ill-fated climate began to rear its ugly head towards Delaware. It brought feelings of anxiety and fear; the hurricane Irene had arrived Delaware and which culminated in a flee for refuge. These whirlwinds of crises increasingly threatened to shatter this intended rosy experience. Even though the guests departed, lots of telephone calls, prayers, encouragement and support were extended to them as an expression of love and loyalty.

Natalie, being the little girl she is, was rather glad that in the absence of the paternal support of her father which she missed at the time of this event, her loving mother and other family members were there to share the feared experience. What could have been compared with such a presence, imbued with warmth and care and most importantly, a spiritual touch, which activated a will to overcome and not to succumb to the travails of the day?

A lot of lessons were learnt from this amazing experience. The love of family supersedes everything. On the day of the earthquake, hands were joined in agreement, prayers were made, feelings were shared which brought a sense of easiness and hope. The memories of strategic moments shared together, both in good and bad, to Natalie, serve as mementos, precious gifts that money could not buy.

Dr. Odilia Osakwe

My family lately

Mom and I on the mother's day

Reading a speech I prepared
for mom on her birthday

August 9, 2011
The Arrival

Today, the rain showered in Delaware as if there was a storm. It rained so hard that we just had to stay inside and wait for it to stop. It made my day a dull one. This feeling did not take away my joy because I knew I was expecting my loved ones. So, I just stayed and waited. Hours later, my mom's jeep pulled up with Auntie Odiche and my cousins, Maurine and Kathy arrived. They were picked up by my mom from the arrival. I ran outside to embrace then and to render a warm welcome.

They were welcomed by Erin and Sam my brothers. They all seemed really happy to see my brothers and me. I was happy to see them and especially my auntie since I haven't seen her for so long. It was a joyful experience. They all sat down in one of our sitting rooms looking tired. Mom served them some special food she had prepared. They settled down and had their dinner that we spent most of the day preparing. As their baggage was taken to the rooms, they looked around the house while I followed them around with auntie holding my arms. My cousins immediately noticed the new trampoline and got very excited. My mom relaxed with her sister in conversation while I talked with my cousins. I am glad to day is the wonder day, the arrival of my special gusests. I can't wait to see what we will do together tomorrow.

August 10, 2011
The Great Cousins-
Maurine and I

I am exactly the same age as Maurine. We were both born in Nashville, Tennessee in an apartment where my mom, Auntie Odiche, my mom's sister and Auntie Rose, Maurine's mom once lived. We have a bond and this started right from birth. It grows everyday and I am glad that she is here to stay a little longer. We are all happy to see each other because, we only see once in a year and for only two or three days during the Thanksgiving holidays when my mom's brother, Uncle Andrew usually brings his family over for a get together. Maurine and I had always longed to be together. We really craved for this opportunity and which never came till now. We see ourselves growing and have always hoped that we do not grow out of our childhood without having to share our stories together. Even though we made occasional telephone conversations, we thought we needed something more than that. We had the chance to meet during my auntie's wedding. We had a good time but this was also short-lived because it was less than a week. Mom, my other two brothers and I had paid a visit to New York where they live but that was on few occasions and each time, it was like a small funfair for all of us. This time, they stayed much longer. Kathy, the other cousin is seven, while Erin my brother is eight, Sam is the youngest and only four years old.

I made breakfast for everyone this morning. I mostly like to prepare eggs in omelets. Luckily, my cousins love it too. Everyone seemed to enjoy their breakfast and I am pleased. Erin has two friends, Cyril and Richard. They visited the house this time making the house even fuller. We played Just Dance 2, War, Table Soccer and then watched Degrassi altogether. We had lots of fun. Now, I played with a bigger number and especially my cousins. This is very exciting for me. That is why I could not sleep well the night before their coming when my mom gave me a short notice so that it would be a surprise. My cousins, Maurine and Kathy also told me that they slept for only two hours because of over excitement.

After, Erin's friends had gone, auntie gave all the kids in the house, english and math work to do. We worked in our workbooks. My mom allowed us to play on the trampoline after studies. We played for about an hour then, ate ice cream after. Erin gave Cyril a message on his back in writing. While this was happening, his friend dialed numbers on the phone. As soon as he was done dialing the numbers, he went back home to be with his parents. A few minutes later, the police called asking if things were ok. I am glad they did not rather come because that call should not have been made in the first place. It is still not known who made the call between the two.

August 11, 2011
The Airplane Experience

Auntie always woke up in the morning, earlier than others. She often came over to our beds to check on us after she woke up. The first thing we always did when we woke up was to gather for morning prayers and Bible readings. I learnt good lessons during these times. Breakfast was great just as usual. My dad, sent a text today ".... I love you Natalie" he typed. I always love it when he sends word to me. He sends messages to both Erin and Ivery often. He always wants to make sure we are alright. We love him so much! We miss him.

The kids went on the trampoline together. Erin's friends, Cyril and Richard came over as usual. A little while, Cyril started asking me lots of questions that I rather would not answer. To make him stop asking me these questions, I decided to play a funny song on the piano for Maurine and Cyril.

I thought it would be funny to make the match and play the song for them. Maurine stopped me from playing even before I could finish. Funny! What a big joke!

My auntie always reminded me of making my journal entries very often during the day period. I told auntie that I would not be able to bring my journal everywhere. "What if I go to my friend's party or on a journey or flying (I might not be comfortable writing in the air)?" I asked. While I said these things, I remembered something. "When I was eight years old, peoples' seats were switched around in an airplane making me to sit next to two strangers. They smelled like old people," I said. When I said that, my auntie laughed out loud and so hard. Maurine explained that she had that same experience before where she had to be placed in between two strange people in the air plane and nobody agreed to change positions.

August 12, 2014
The Outing

This morning, we read the Bible. My auntie read Psalm 23, The Lord is my Shepherd. I learned from this verse that I should always be bold to call on Jesus in times of danger so that I will not fear. Dad texts again ". . . I love you, Natalie." "I love you too," I replied. He often sends us little reminders about taking care of ourselves well.

I made egg and biscuits for breakfast for everyone and they all enjoyed it. After breakfast, we went to Walmart to buy some supplies. We visited the Macy's too. "Kids, just wait for me here. I am going to rush off to get something," my mom said as she walked away. We then waited for her in the fitting room together with auntie. All the kids are always excited when we are together. We ran all around the store looking for a bathroom to use while auntie was with us. A man working in the store was very kind to us. He showed us the way. "Make a right and go on to the elevator, go upstairs and then walk straight into it," he told auntie. Everyone went upstairs and here mom comes! She was looking at pots.We waited for about half an hour until my mom was done. When everything was packed up and ready to go, my mom drove to the day care and picked up Sam. We then got into the car and mom took us to a Chinese buffet. The food was very delicious. I did not know that my cousin, Kathy was able to eat with sticks. I ate with sticks too. All of us ate lots of crabs. My mom started eating crabs and others then followed. We ate other dishes too. My auntie did not want to eat crabs. How could one's like become another's dislike? The crabs that my mom loves so much, auntie does not?

Kids by the car

Left to right. Auntie Odiche, Natalie,
Kathy (front) Erin (back) mom
(front) going to the store.

Mom dropped me off to my friend's house on our way back from the days' outing to spend a little time with her. At that time, we had not seen each other for a while. Her name is Evie. We have been very good friends for a long time. We had a good time together in her home. When I came back home, my piano teacher was already there waiting. She taught me the song 'I Got a Feeling'. When she was done, mom paid her and she left.

Our Wii game has been keeping us busy. Maurine is a little bit chubby. My auntie insists that she should play it more often to help her lose weight. I usually win the dances with high scores and big gaps whenever I play with all the kids. I was thinking that since I am slim, maybe my body is lighter and easier to move around. The score that one receives depends on how fast that player could match up the dancing moves of the dancer in the game. My favorite is 'Toxic'. Everybody played their turn when it was time. I tried not to play too much so that I could read my books. One of my greatest hobbies is reading. My parents buy lots of books for me and I always make out time for reading them. I have read lots of books, some of which are 'The Key in Chronicles' and 'The Hunger Games' series. The one of 'Michelle Obama-An American Story' by David Colbert told that Michelle Robinson Obama started reading before elementary school and skipped her second grade. She chose reading over sports when she was growing up and I believe, that contributes to her present achievements, popularity and fame.

Reading is my hobby. Having read so many books, it just became very natural that I am writing a book of my own now. I am very happy that an opportunity like this was made possible. I would like for this summer to be a remarkable event in my lifetime. Even though I am eleven years old, I feel very confident that this period of my life will never pass unnoticed. That is my greatest joy!

I admire my mom and auntie when they talked and how they brought up things that happened in the past. Their conversation seemed warm. "How I admire seeing you and auntie chat that way. I am just thinking how it will be by the time we kids grow up. How close are we going to be to each other at the time of my mom's age, just like she and auntie?" I told mom. Mom and auntie have similar eating habits and taste. I have noticed some of my mom's habits in auntie.

I play my piano very often for practice. I practice all the time because I overheard my auntie saying, "if you leave the piano, piano leaves you" To me, this means I have to practice as I learn. My piano teacher comes once a week. My cousins watch me as I play. I really enjoy playing it a lot. Erin has joined the class lately. My mom wants to give both of us an equal chance. I miss my dad, since he went overseas. He is always interested to know how good I play. We talk from time to time anyway. He sends greetings from my cousins at the other side of the world map, Nigeria.

I left the room and went downstairs to get some milk, while on my way back; I noticed a pack of chewing gum on the floor. We went to the Walmart earlier today. When we finished shopping and reached the cashier spot, Erin bought a chewing gum pack (6ft roll) and gave to Kathy. I bought Hershey's chocolate and Maurine bought a candy. My auntie told Kathy not to continue eating her gum. "It is not very healthy and safe to eat too much of it." She wrapped it up in a shopping bag she was holding.

August 13, 2011
The Chewing Gum

We had a gaping huge pile of laundry to get done and everything needed to be separated out according to color semblance. The laundry was huge! But guess what? We jumped at it. We gathered four baskets and then sorted the whole bundle. The job load cleared rapidly since more hands were in the scene. My cousins really worked hard and were very serious sorting and folding the laundry. The whole job was sort of demanding so, we took it very seriously and actually finished in good time. Somebody would be wondering what was going on if they caught sight of how these clothes were flying into the different baskets. I learned from this experience that working together is important in life.

I am very glad I have graduated from elementary school, ready to move up to one level higher. I will be going to the middle school to the 6th grade when school re-opens. Sad I will be dropping my old friends and making new ones. My mom had ordered long-sleeved shirts and trying it on alone gave me a feeling. You cannot beat it! This is a sign that I am going close to my teenage age and this is important to me.

Auntie made a pot of stir-fried rice with lots of vegetables in it. Even though it is called a healthy dinner, I really do not mind those vegetables. I do not care about them. I prefer plain rice. Auntie was a little bit worried and did not like my choice at all. She felt it was strange that I said that. I announced that this would go into my journal entry. "Then, be prepared because, it is going to be our daily meal nowadays," mom said. "I hope not!" I said in my mind. In the midst of all of that, I took some and ate for dinner just to please auntie and mom. I wonder why my cousin, Maurine loves it. I am learning to eat them now because it is really healthy and this is what I need to stay healthy.

I noticed an empty pack of chewing gum on the floor. I thought it was the pack of this gum that Erin had bought for Kathy from Walmart. I picked it up to see what was inside. "Empty!" I exclaimed. Erin was just walking. As he passed by me, he started to watch me to know why I was curious. "Who ate all the gum?" I asked. "Kathy chewed and swallowed it all," he replied. I covered my face. This gum is 6ft in length which means, it is longer than the whole of my height (I am more than 5 ft). I got worried. Then I explained to Erin for him to understand that chewing gums don't digest. We were all worried. A few minutes later, Kathy came downstairs. "What happened to the chewing gum, Kathy?" I asked with surprise. She watched my eyes and knew there was danger. "I ate and swallowed all," she replied with fear. "Please Natalie, do not tell auntie".

Later on in the day, Cyril and Richard came again. It rained and rained today. Their hairs and their bodies were soaked wet when they came to the door. We let them in. We all played in the basement. It was like they zipped out again because they only stayed for about twenty minutes.

Few hours later, I told auntie that Kathy ate the whole gum that Erin bought for her. "Kathy said I should not tell you but if I don't her life may be in danger. I am more interested in her safety," I told auntie. I read the chewing gum label and it says it is 6 ft. long. We were all scared and prayed on Kathy for healing. During this time, Kathy was so terrified. This was in the night time. "I am tired and I want to sleep. Auntie, I am tired, I want to sleep," she said in a shaky voice. Auntie visited the internet immediately. Auntie said that the gum was huge that was why she was concerned. If it was small, she would not worry. After a long searching, she said that the information obtained from the internet was "confounding" and that nothing was "conclusive". She sent all of us, the kids to bed "Now that everyone is sleeping, I pray for Kathy's health, Amen!" I said while on my bed waiting to sleep.

August 14, 2011
The Special Touch

We all woke up to carry out our morning routines before getting ready for church, because it was Sunday. "Auntie, why should we only pray in Natalie's room instead of mine?" Erin asked. "We could switch now," auntie said. She again repeated that Erin's room would be the new venue for our morning prayer meetings. Erin was happy to go to church. He caught auntie's attention and started to explain what usually happened in the church as we were getting ready. "Mostly, the preacher would stand in the pulpit to say many things about Jesus while people sat down and listened to him.

Kids between 3rd and 5th grade stayed together in a separate room where they saw comics about Jesus," he said in excitement. Erin again said that church was fun.

Yesterday, I heard my auntie say she is an early riser that she could not sleep beyond her early waking time. Because my mom told her about being late to church before, auntie promised that this would not repeat. She made that commitment to herself to make sure that everyone went to church early. Waking up early is a routine for her anyway. She woke every one up to have a shower and to prepare breakfast for all. That did not help at all because mom still did not wake up on time. She had a troubled sleep the night before. She had to get Sam ready and chase him around to eat breakfast after all the time used in dressing him up.

Everyone got dressed and was ready for church. I was wearing my green, white and black plaid dress with shiny black tights and golden brown shoes. Maurine wore a long sleeved silky blue, white and black striped gown while Kathy wore a floral dress on a white—embroidered shiny white shoe. Erin just wore a simple shirt on three-quartered pants with snickers. My mom and auntie looked very nice too; I like their taste in fashion. My mom pulled over, I stepped into the car, buckled my belt along with others. We left thirty minutes late. I saw my auntie's face, she was worried, really worried over our being late.

Three minutes after we arrived the church, the fire alarm started to ring with an announcement asking everybody to leave the church. I panicked and was wondering how everybody could leave the church. I did not know what to do. Interestingly, some of the church officials told us that it was just a false alarm. As we stepped inside the church, Maurine and I went to the same room while Erin and Kathy went to another room. Sam went to the toddlers' room while auntie and mom went inside the church sanctuary, the main church hall. When the church dismissed, I did not see neither mom nor auntie so, Maurine and I went over to the toddlers room to pick up Sam and to see if we could meet mom coming to pick Sam since I did not get a response after making several calls to her cell phone. I then saw auntie coming out with mom's purse. It seemed like they were making a private prayer. We all waited till mom came. The rain would not stop so, mom walked to her car with her umbrella just alone so that she could get her car while we waited for her in the front. She then pulled over and let everyone in. I stepped into the car, buckled my belt and the others did the same. We put Sam in his car seat and got him well buckled up. We went home.

It rained and rained. It rained cats and dogs today. I asked my auntie. Why did my mom move from Tennessee to Delaware? "Delaware is not better than Tennessee because it rains every day here?" "Not necessarily, it does not make Delaware better. You cannot compare two states only based on their climates," she said in laughter. "Why then did you move to Delaware? I am concerned because it rains very often here and this is supposed to be summer!" I asked curiously. "To move in with your daddy," she replied. "I am asking because she had mentioned that she does not mind the rain, auntie," I continued.

When we arrived home, we could still not come out of the car. The rain still hit very hard. Mom suggested that we wait for the rain to stop, but auntie would rather come out. So mom placed the car well closer to the garage door so that auntie could come out. Auntie brought out Sam very carefully. Then everyone rushed out. Mom backed up her car and then came out with an umbrella.

Auntie prepared lunch for everyone. "Now, our dining table is filled up with people these days," I rejoiced. Everybody spread out over the round dining table, eyeing each other. "I like this!" I said in excitement. After lunch, we went to the sitting room to play 'Just Dance' on the Wii. We usually danced in pairs; Maurine and I, Kathy and Erin. We gave my auntie a special invitation to come and play the dance with us. This time Maurine played with auntie. Auntie was winning and this made Kathy was so happy. "My auntie is winning!" Kathy announced with joy. "No it is my auntie," Erin replied. "No it is myyyy auntie," Kathy said back forcefully. "No, she is my mom's sister," Erin shouts back to her. "She is my dad's sister," Kathy gets back to him. Kathy got angry and held on to Erin and then cried. Auntie laughed and laughed. She is really the auntie of Erin and Kathy. She is my mom's sister and Kathy dad's sister as well and so she is related to both of them in the same way. None of them could have more claim over her!

Playing the Wii games

Playing Wii games in style

Later on, Cyril zipped in again. He was so much soaked in the rain when he rang the doorbell. When mom came out and he asked for Erin, mom told him that he could not see Erin. "Why not, why not, why not, why not," he replied in an unfriendly way and quickly and walked off into the woods. I always wondered why he disappeared into the woods because that was not the first time. The other day, Cyril and Richard came over again. This time only auntie was around. They were soaked in the rain with fishing rods in their hands. "You cannot see Erin today," auntie instructed. "Why not, why not," they replied in their usual style and walked off into the woods. She locked the door and we all came in.

Auntie made a good dinner and we ate to our satisfaction. Mom made the announcement that we would have a special prayer session by 8pm in the night. We all got prepared for this very special occasion. During prayer, we started with the songs that mom had chosen for us to sing. After, we then sang my own choice of song. During prayer, mom and auntie started saying different things at the same time. They were really rattling in a confused manner. It seemed like the Holy Spirit was really present, hovering around us. It probably touched them but how come I am not doing the same? My auntie went out of control in the spirit. She was screaming and praying very hard while we sang and sang. "Hey, Heeey, Hey, Heeey," she screamed. Everyplace is seemingly on fire with this 'Holy Spirit performance'. The noise got worse. I was surprised. As auntie screamed aloud, I and Maurine tried our best not to laugh, but we could not help not laughing so we giggled repeatedly but stuck our heads in between our legs to vent out and not stifle from it. We did not want it to seem like we were having fun in the presence of the Holy Spirit. We would not like to be noticed as well. Maurine said she thought that my mom and auntie were going to have a fight when my auntie was screaming with Holy Spirit-filled impulses and going close to her. I figured she was just laying her hands over mom in prayer. Mom was lost in her vibrations. These vibrations could set off a nice drumming if it was only brought close to her body. I was trying to make sense of what was really happening all this time. "I should be really used to this so that I can behave better next time," I told myself. My mom then led us in prayer. She prayed for a long time. We sang more gospel songs. We prayed for my dad's safe return from his journey. Every one of us gave a special prayer asking for God's grace and mercies.

August 15, 2011
Unexpected Displacement

Around 11:47 am I got hungry and asked auntie if I could have breakfast (we did not want to eat earlier). She decided to make pancakes for everyone. When she was making it, I watched her so that I could learn to cook the way she did. She explained that the pancake needed to have an optimal "consistency" in order to be able to keep the form of a flat and smoothly rounded pancake. I watched as she added water to the batter. She then added butter to the pan and poured the pancake mix as well. At first, Maurine didn't think she liked pancakes but when she tried auntie's she instantly loved them. When I ate my pancake, I could tell that it was a work well done. We all ate and I washed the dishes. My cousins and I usually took turns in washing the dishes.

Mom had gone out earlier. She asked all of us to help unload everything from the car as she returned. She usually shops on her way back from work. All the kids rushed out and helped to bring out all the bags from my mom's car. It worked out so well with more hands on deck.

After that, we played the Wii games. My mom, requested to play a dance game on the Wii against my auntie. They chose 'Holiday'. During the dance, everyone voted on who they wanted to cheer. I and Erin chose to cheer for my mom. Auntie said she would cheer for my mom too. She said she would because she is her sister. Funny! Maurine, the only one present at the time cheered for my auntie. After the dance, they were so tired. I think they need to do more of those for exercise mostly.

Mom went to her shopping bags that we had pulled out of her car earlier. As she unpacked the bags, I saw a black dress with floral patterns. That was for me. She got me a navy blue two-piece swimsuit. I tried them on and they were exactly my size. That made me happy. I went to my room and hung them up in my closet. I knew she was preparing for an event coming ahead of us. She got some clothing for Maurine and Kathy too.

My cousins always got stuck with the TV especially when the Ned's Declassified would be on. It was always hard to get them off during these times. Kathy is very independent. Whenever she was with my iPod touch, she would stay on it all day and preferred to be alone this time. Her ears got plugged with an earphone every minute, I mean keeping the ear phone on her ear every hour until my auntie reminded her that it is time for a change.

My auntie dismissed everyone to their studies as the evening approached. She gave each of us different assignments both mostly in English, Math or book reading and writing. My auntie is well-educated. She has a doctoral degree and you could tell because she likes to talk about school and books. She writes articles and publishes them in the city magazines. My mom is educated and intelligent too. I overheard them talking about how my mom was so brilliant during her school years. While in the primary school, her great intelligence led to skipping a grade level. She was moved directly from grade three to grade five. While in grade five, she became a classmate to her elder brother, Uncle Andrew. That made Uncle Andrew very jealous. He was no longer her friend as from that time because he felt she came to challenge him in his class which he thought should not be because she was younger and did not belong there. She cried more in the house because Uncle Andrew was jealous and would pick on her every slightest fault leaving my grandmother, their mother a handful of problems to deal with. They laughed and laughed. This reminds me of Michelle Robinson Obama skipping her second grade in elementary school as told in the book 'Michelle Obama-An American Story'. She was okay after that, but my mom paid for hers. Funny.

My grandmother, Mrs. Dawn was a school principal while my grandfather, Dr. Daniel was an academic doctor. My auntie said that she really wanted to respond to his desire that was a part of the reason why she became a doctor as him. According to auntie, by the time she rounded off her doctoral degree, he had died. "I then dedicated my doctoral work to my deceased father," she began. "My dad inspired me mostly and that helped a lot in obtaining this higher degree." In the front page of her dissertation she wrote "To my loving parents. You are my life and heat. Father (named), you inspired my decision to obtain a doctoral degree but did not live to embrace it"

During studies, auntie would always send all the kids to separate spots in the house to help them to be more serious in their reading and to avoid distractions. "Kathy talks quite a bit. It is really good that she gets her own space." I said. When my auntie assigned their reading, she went upstairs. About five minutes later, Kathy came upstairs to put her book back in the shelf and was ready for the iPod touch again. Funny! Auntie sent her back to her reading. She read for only five minutes before this time. She was mostly interested in the iPod.

Twenty minutes later, I went to the basement to get my poster board that I had used for the District Science Fair competition to show to my auntie. As I passed through the kitchen, everyone circled around me like a swarm of bees to ask me if they could have some snack. I told them that I was not in charge but referred them to auntie. They refused to ask her, knowing that their request might not be granted especially when they ask for too much. "How about me?" I have not asked for snacks too," I walked away. Auntie then came down and answered their request when she overheard their demands. I went back upstairs and Erin followed me so as to inform auntie that he had finished reading his book and how his head had been hurting him. Auntie said he could have a break from reading.

Mom and dad believe so much in fitness. They want us to always participate in fitness activities, so, I had been in cheerleading and other activities. Erin had enrolled to join a football team so he still goes for a two-hour football practice, three times in a week. He came back today with a head shield and a shoulder pad and decided not to take them off. He walked around the house with his shoulders raised high with pride because he loved the new football outfit. You could hardly see his face when the head shield was on. My brother looked all puffed up and huge inside his new outfit. He was looking for someone to play with. "Who will play with me?" I don't mind playing inside the house, it does not matter where we are so long as we can play" he said as he paced round the house. He just loved his outfit, that's all. He got tired after circling the house and finding no one to play with and then later on, agreed to remove those.

I took my cousins upstairs to help me in the folding of my clothes. They were excited to help me; not only to fold my clothes, but to organize the whole room. In a short while, mom brought lots of socks for us to sort out. "There you go!" she said with a smiling face as she dumped the clothes. It was overwhelming and fun at the same time. "It is your responsibility to help mom, make it fun," auntie said as she sat down beside me. Then the idea of sock war came up. "Oh! We could play sock war then," I said to my cousins. At least, I have my cousins around to play with me with after all." While alone with Erin, it would not have been this much fun like it has become now. So I kept this new plan in my mind waiting for the right time to start this 'war'.

August 16, 2011
The Sock War

My auntie was downstairs in her quiet time. I grabbed a couple of photo albums and showed her. She screamed and wondered how my mom had changed over the years, because, she was looking so youthful in those photos. I did see how I had changed from being a baby going towards my present age. I saw myself in a picture taken in front of a limousine together with my cousins, two years ago. This reminded me of something in the past. We attended my auntie's wedding in Atlanta, Georgia two years ago. On the wedding day, we discovered that we would be late as the limousine wasn't there yet. Two ladies that were delivering flowers for the wedding offered to take, Kathy, me and other adults to the church where the wedding was to take place, because we were among the few that were left who waited for the limousine. As we arrived at the wedding place, we saw the limousine behind us with Erin, my mom and Maurine inside. They came out of the limousine and explained to me what happened. Anyway I enjoyed the ride later because, after the church wedding all the kids, mostly the nieces and nephews of auntie and auntie's husband, uncle Dede were all in the limousine and were taken to the reception hall. We had fun. It is an event I will not forget because that was another meeting place for all of my mother's family living in the United States. I met with all of my cousins, Auntie Odiche and her husband; Uncle Andrew and his wife.

Left to right. Chi, Juju, David (in front), Maurine and Natalie at the wedding in Atlanta, Georgia

The lawn mowers drove by. "How much for all of these?" mom asked the mowers as she waved her hand over whole area in the front yard. "Twenty dollars," they replied. Auntie agreed to pay but forgot to give them the money as soon as they finished. She came out later, to find them standing and waiting helplessly for a long time. "I am sorry! I am sorry I am sorry!" she rained apologies on them. It was funny because, she kept going on and on. I laughed. It amused them as well.

We went upstairs to complete the folding of our laundry. It was mainly socks but the heap was as high as a small stool and as wide as my piano key board. "It is time to launch this sock war which has been my new idea," I said. I and my cousins started playing a toss game with these socks called 'sock war'. As soon as auntie approached us, we quickly switched from sock war game to work. She did not know we took out some time to play our sock war but immediately resumed and pretended that nothing happened when she looked behind. This was going on several times without her knowledge as she backed us to work on the internet. Whenever she looked back, we pretended to be working. Funny! We continued to repeat doing these and later on revealed the trick we played on her.

Erin has been keeping quiet today. He can really be moody when he wants. I am glad that the popping of the popcorn captured his attention and he ended up coming downstairs to join us since he loved pop corns. Funny! Maurine, the plumpy one, loaded herplate heavier. She does like food. Maurine likes to ask for extras. I asked my auntie when Erin's friend would come again. "You miss them and their trouble right?" she said. "I just wanted to know," I replied.

The kids went to jump on the trampoline with auntie watching. Auntie was saying she needed us especially, Maurine to be jumping on the trampoline since she needed to lose weight. We jumped for a while and took breaks from time to time. Erin brought a ball which we tossed as we jumped.

I remembered that the next day would be my tutoring session so I rushed upstairs to get my assignments updated. "I should have no excuses," I said to myself.

During dinner, we circled the dining table as usual and had a good talk over dinner. Erin said we had the second best grass in the neighborhood but had to do something to the first in order to take over the first position! We said no, that's cheating.

We had a sock war after dinner. During this game, we all ganged up against Maurine and she kept loosing. She became the 'forever looser'.

Mom returned from work with Sam because she normally picks him up from the day care on her way home. Erin kept himself busy struggling and pleading for Sam to permit him to play his game of choice as he was tired of Sam's Mario game. Whenever Sam comes back from the daycare with mom, then, we start hearing "Mario—Luigi! Mario—Luigi! Mario—Luigi! I want my Mario and Luigi! Sam draws everybody's attention and keeps going until the game is turned on. He stays on it for most of the evening. Mom, in a way likes it since it gives her some break to focus on other duties around the house. On the days that Sam stays home like when mom could not drop him off to the daycare place, playing any type of game on our television is usually difficult because Sam stays on it all day and will be interested in nothing else. I wanted to play a game too but we all had to go to watch Erin's football game today. For the first time, the four of us (my mom and all her kids) left the house and the house became quiet and peaceful according to auntie who stayed back with my two cousins. She said the house was really quiet.

Mom got back from the grocery. We saw the push pops she bought. Everybody was excited and wanted to take each. All of us so much desired the push pops. My mom said that candy could be poison when abused. As soon as she said that, Kathy lost interest in candy immediately. Auntie laughed so hard. We explained to Auntie how the push pops works. We showed her. Mom demanded a change in behavior before we could have the push pops. She believed we made noise (sometimes there could be noise because we are just happy and satisfied with ourselves). We rushed and washed all the dishes in a minute. "How they could wash the dishes in just a minute, I do not know!" mom said surprisingly. "They really need push pops," Erin said as he approached mom. "What else can we do to change so that we could have our share of the push pops?" he asked mom. Mom remained quiet. We then tried to be quiet and not talk too much as usual. We latter got the push pops.

The pizza that mom ordered arrived. We all got our share of it. Sam asked for pizza and marshmallows. My mom gave him one slice of pizza and two marshmallows. Sam ran to his plate, snatched the two marshmallows leaving the pizza behind. Funny! "Why did he ask for pizza in the first place?" I asked.

Kathy told us how she felt like she saw a piece of gum in her urine. "Auntie, when I was in the bathroom, I felt like I saw a little piece of gum come out" she explained. "Are you sure?" asked auntie. "I just feel like there was gum" she replied in a tiny shaky voice. Her mind was still stuck on the gum she swallowed the other day. Everybody laughed. I jumped up and down laughing on the floor.

Later on in the day, Cyril and Richard came over asking for Erin. Auntie told them that Erin was at the football practice. Auntie asked them if their parents knew where they had been to. "No, our parents don't care where we go as long as we are able to reach home by midnight," Cyril answered while walking to and forth, pacing the floor in front of our front door. Auntie let them go home. Erin is a different type of person. He does not walk freely outdoors like they do. Mom makes sure he is always inside. She has a lot to keep him busy anyway. They are really not his very close friends. They just saw him somewhere and started to visit him.

As we helped my mom unload the trunk we heard someone scream out the word frog!. We saw it when we went to the garage. I panicked and ran inside along with my cousins. I remembered that we had a job to do so I told Erin to get a broom and hit the frog. As Erin was hitting the frog with a broom stick, Maurine and I ran outside to get the remaining groceries. When everything was inside we closed the garage door and ran inside.

August 17, 2011
The-Sprinkler—over -Trampoline Idea

In the morning Erin and I decided to play a game called Super Mario Wii. In the game, the killer is usually the winner. Erin attempted so hard to kill my person in the game. He would lift my character up and throw me into a volcano full of lava. Fortunately for Erin, he won a round. I got really upset with Erin because he kept screaming out "I am a killer!" his screaming filled the whole house with so much noise. Auntie came downstairs wondering. "Who is the person dying?" she asked.

"It was just a game, don't mind him auntie, nobody is dying," I said.

Later on in the day we asked auntie if we could go on the trampoline, auntie refused because it was too hot outside. We begged and pleaded until she finally allowed us to go outside. After five minutes, we realized that auntie was right that it was really too hot outside. We went back in. Later on, I found an idea; I called my mom and asked her if we could use the sprinkler. She allowed us. We changed into our swimsuits and rushed outside. Erin was interested in the trampoline not the sprinkler so he did not want to join us. It seems like he was outnumbered. He didn't want to get involved with too many "girly things". So three of us went upstairs and dressed in our swimsuits. Maurine came with a smaller size swimsuit and she didn't know that. She had to depend on auntie for wearing that because she needed help to put it on. Auntie helped her to fit it on her body. Awesome! We dashed out into the front yard and had our fun. It was a big blast. We wet and soaked ourselves to our satisfaction. I am so much enjoying this summer.

I found another idea. I brought the sprinkler near the trampoline to make water spray over the trampoline as we jumped. We then got inside the trampoline and the sprinkler sprayed water to cool us down while we jumped. Erin had a sock problem. He loves his socks and would not take them off. He loves wearing it around the house, no matter what the weather says. It would cause problems for him especially with my new sprinkler-over-trampoline idea. He wanted to take his socks to the trampoline, but it would not make any sense taking it because of the sprinkler that could wet the sock easily. Now, his socks could get soaked and messy while jumping in the trampoline. He gave up at last. I think he still prefers to have the fun instead. He pulled off his socks and jumped into the trampoline to get wet.

As soon as we got into the trampoline, Maurine started to jump up and down with so much energy and happiness. We couldn't jump well until she stopped, since she had the most weight. Erin was the most affected because he jumped close to her and especially as she jumped so hard with lots of energy. Erin could be thrown into the air easily. We all sat down to rest and Maurine was still jumping so we bounced along with her, up and down until she agreed to sit down along with us. It's a good thing that we had the sprinkler with us because it gave nice cooling as we bounced to our pleasure.

We got really tired so we lay down on the trampoline and looked at the clouds. Erin told us that Maurine's body jiggled too much when she jumped that she should make it stop. Maurine asked Erin not to make that comment anymore. She told him to hold off on any conversation relating to her "whatever" body. Maurine would only let Kathy see her that way since they are sisters. Kathy did not even accept the offer! She didn't want to look at Maurine's body in any special way at all. Maurine got a bit mad and insisted that Kathy should look at her body to find out if it was really giggling. Everyone laughed so hard. We dragged and dragged. Evie, my best friend came over. We went over to the trampoline again. We locked Erin out because he was not wearing a shirt. He was bare-bodied. He went inside and complained to auntie but was never able to play again since he refused to wear his shirt. Inside the trampoline, we made up a game called 'Rocks'. Here, a stupid girl thinks that the fake rocks are real. So she was deceived. All of us got to pretend as the stupid girl. Three people lay down. "Oh look at these rocks; I am going to fall on them" one girl said. She then fell on them with the mind that they are rocks even though they are real people.

We went downstairs to play sock war. Erin showed up to auntie. "Auntie, I can hardly hear with this ear! Kathy hit me with a sock!" Auntie stopped the sock wars because of that complain.

August 18, 2011
Trampoline for Sam

In the morning, we all went to Erin's room for prayer to satisfy his request from auntie the other day. My auntie told me that the time when she would return to Toronto city, that I would be in charge, which means I am going to take over and organize Bible and prayer meetings for the family. As we were talking, Sam showed up from the bedroom asking for help. I walked away with him.

When I came back into the room I saw everyone reading their Bibles. I got out my Bible and joined them. When we finished reading our scriptures, we prayed for my mom, my brothers and me After our prayers, we talked about heaven. The story is so lovely that I started longing for heaven. I really want to go to heaven. My auntie described heaven as a place where you are always happy and how you never get tired or hungry. When she said that, I was confused because I was so used to eating and sleeping. She told me that our spirits in heaven will be different from that of humans after we die. That helped my understanding of what heaven will be like.

Auntie was browsing through her writings in the net. She brought up one piece of her writings that was published in one of the Toronto city magazines. The writing had the picture of a drink beside an empty chip bag stuffed with broccoli. "Weird! broccoli with chips! What kind of writing is this auntie?" Kathy began to ask. "Kathy, is auntie famous because of all these?" Erin asks. "Just fifty percent famous" she replied. Funny!

The thought of jumping in the trampoline came up. Maurine is the most eager one. She always wants to go immediately but as auntie delayed the time to a later time she screamed regretfully. We tried to strike a deal with auntie. She allowed us to go by 6pm. She said it would be hot before 6 pm. Maurine declared that she would prefer 5pm regardless. Auntie then accepted this suggestion for the sake of peace. She allowed 5pm. "4:30pm?" Maurine demanded again. It was 4pm then. Auntie asked if it was fair enough that she moved it up to 5pm from 6pm, Maurine said it was not fair. Then auntie decided to move it back to 6pm "since auntie was not fair" auntie continues. YOU ARE FAIR! YOU ARE FAIR! YOU ARE FAIR!" Everybody screamed.

"There is one more problem. Who knows what the problem is?" Auntie asked. I raised my hand—Sam. "Oh! Yes!" said auntie. What will we do about Sam? "We can buy a small tent for him since he is under age," said Kathy. "Auntie, do you have a driver's license?" Erin asks. "Yes," she said. Then you can use my daddy's car while he is a way to go to either my friend's house to borrow a small trampoline or buy one from the store. He handed auntie his phone. "Text him," Erin said. Auntie refused the kind offer. "Auntie, another way out is to remove Maurine from jumping the trampoline since she is heavy weight to avoid throwing the little Sam off the net," he continued. "No, No" Maurine screamed. Erin started telling everyone that Maurine almost killed him on the trampoline.

He said that Maurine jumped so high that he almost fell out of the trampoline. He started telling everyone that Maurine was so big that if Sam went on the trampoline with us she would make him fly out of the trampoline.

Auntie went down stairs to the basement and found Maurine all by herself. When she asked, Maurine said they were making a mockery of her— Erin always teased her on her heavy weight impact on the trampoline that could throw anyone off the tent only with a little force. Kathy earlier warned Erin that his loose tongue could hurt Maurine's feelings. And it really did this time. Funny!

Erin became so interested in the sprinkler idea. He had pressed so much for the sprinkler to be brought near the trampoline. His constant demand for the sprinkler to be brought to the trampoline wore auntie out. He kept mom on the phone to make sure she is convinced. Auntie allowed him. We soaked ourselves and drenched in water. I had an idea, I went to a place where there was a little hollow on the ground with no grass and sprayed water there. Soon it became mud. I started to jump in it and felt good about it. Just a little mess! "Look I am jumping up and down in the muddy puddles!" I screamed out. Everyone rushed over, they all wanted to jump in muddy puddles as well. Soon, we made about two muddy puddles and jumped in them. Maurine smacked me with my green swimming tube and said she won bonus points for that!

Erin jumped with joy when he knew that we were having sweet potatoes for lunch. It is his favorite. He took it to a little place undisturbed so that he could eat to his pleasure.

While in the shower, Maurine knocked on the secret door leading to my bedroom to the bathroom. I was asking to know who was knocking but there was no answer. I continued with her shower. She thought of an idea, she put a whoopee cushion covered with a blanket and opened the door to scare me. I know she was seeking for attention. I have not had people trying to play with me in my shower. It is my cousins of course!

My mom is trying to make us eat healthy now-a-days, so she replaced our regular two percent milk with fat free milk. The fat free milk tastes just neutral in my opinion and it was probably made tasteless because of the all the unhealthy part that were taken off in order to make it healthy. My mom likes to buy a lot of organic stuff like organic lollipops, organic sugar, organic milk, and even organic beef jerky. I hate it! It has no taste to it! Everything is organic down to burger. I told my auntie that there is this idea called 'unintended consequence'. Let me explain. Sometimes people do half research on a food product and later on, only to find out more information about this product to share with the public to be mindful of. For example, people used to say that diet soda was the best "drink diet soda". Then, when scientists did the extra research, they found out that diet soda can lead to a certain type of cancer. What I am trying to say is that today they will say that organic stuff is good for you but tomorrow they will tell you not to use it anymore. Maurine said she is tired of the healthy stuff too. She doesn't like it but had to eat it for her own good. She would put all the toppings; cheese, ketchup, pickles to mask the taste of the organic burger meat.

August 19, 2011
Questions about Heaven

I was the one to wake up first. Suddenly, I heard a strong blast. I jumped out of the bed and rushed downstairs. It appears auntie touched the wrong button of the musical instrument and the volume went extremely high. She apologized and laughed the same time when she saw me. She was enjoying a gospel music and danced along praising God. She kept one song on repeat. I guess she loves it because it kept playing over and over again while she sang along. We all gave her the space. When she was done singing to her satisfaction, she called out "everybody, come downstairs" we rushed down and had our Bible study and morning prayers. She asked us questions about yesterday to know if we understood anything. And we gave our different responses. Since she told us about heaven, we continued to wonder and asked her more questions still on this topic.

"In heaven can you fly? If so, will every one fly all at once? Are we going to bump into each other? Is it possible for everyone to walk? Are we going to be angels? Are there churches in heaven?" I asked. "Do we have to earn the wings? Are we going to become angels? Kathy asks. "Are there clouds in heaven? Are we going to be able to use the bathroom? Do we earn money?" Maurine asks.

Erin takes over with the questioning. "What does our teacher mean when she said we get lots of treasures in heaven? Are we going to get lots of gold? In heaven do we just fly? I want fly so badly but air planes don't count" Erin said. "Why does it not count?" Auntie asked. "It does not count because, you are just sitting there and just flying inside the air plane not in the air. Did Jesus own a horse when he was in heaven?" Do we own horses in heaven?" Erin continues. Auntie told him it is not possible. "Alright. The horse costs little money. How will my daddy not buy one for me? And again.

Mom said I can never have a horse." Where are you going to ride and keep it?" she asked.

Erin said when he gets married, that he does not want to have kids but his mom kept bordering him about having one. He explains that he does not want to have kids when he grows up because mom said that having kids is a full-time job. Auntie wondered why he is thinking that way because he is a kid himself and a full-time job for somebody else too.

Erin then recited his poem to auntie.

Animals
Beavers have teeth so animals eat wheat
Birds can fly and bush babies make you cry
Erin

The seasons
In the summer the grass is green
In the summer we get lots of tree
In the summer the sun is gold
But in the winter, it is really cold
In the winter we get lots of snow
In the winter Christmas is coming
Ho ho
In the winter we make ginger bread

But in the fall leaves fall in your head
In the fall the weeds are new
In the fall the sky is blue
In the fall
A . . . choo!
In the spring, its allergy season
But I don't know the reason
In the spring, there are lots of clovers,
And then we start all over
Erin

August 20, 2011
Evie's Birthday

I will expand my storyline to include an outside activity that I had on this wonderful day. It is the little time I spent with Evie, my best friend on her birthday. I am doing this because, unexpectedly, it became a part my experience.

The word 'birthday' constantly echoed in my head as I was so much in expectation and could not wait for it to come through. Eventually, at last, it was time to get prepared for a trip to my friend, Evie. The evening before, I made my clothing selections and sent it to my mom for approval. She made some suggestions and I got ready for the trip.

"I am certainly going to miss my cousins," I said. I wish this birthday came in another day other than these days that they are spending with me. Evie is my best friend and so I wanted to spend some time with her as well. We have lots of items in our 'to do list' and I hoped we could get through it. "I had really been looking forward to this fateful day". Evie's birthday outdoor activity was planned to take place the next day. The time for the departure of my auntie and cousins gradually approached. They will be leaving next week and my wonderful summer will be approaching its end and of course, school is going to resume shortly," *I said in my mind.*

I woke up today around 6:50am because, It was time for me to leave. But before then, while everyone else were still sleeping, I wondered around the house for about twenty minutes packing up all my extra essentials. Then I went to the laundry room to get out my swimsuit, it was still in the washing cycle. I told my mom that my swimsuit wasn't dry yet and that I had to go to Evie's house in less than thirty minutes. She took out my swimsuit and put it in the dryer. After ten minutes, my swimsuit was done drying and I put it on under my clothes. I called Evie's house and asked her if the parents could pick me up since I was done gathering my things. When Evie's dad came to pick me up, I told my mom and cousins goodbye and headed out.

It was a long drive to the place, about an hour and a half to Rehoboth Beach. To pass time, we played our Nintendo DS's, listened to music and talked. When we saw the sign 'Rehoboth Beach', everybody cheered. Evie's mom drove into the parking lot and told us to help unload the trunk. We went up the sandy walk way leading to the beach then picked our spot and sat down. We grabbed our swimsuits and got ready. "You could go in the water," Mrs. Kamil (Evie's mom) said. Everyone rushed over there. Evie and Callie grabbed the boogie boards and went over to the water. For the first few minutes, we stayed around the curved water edge. The rocks pushed up against my legs as the curves hit the ground. After five curving waves, I went into the water the more. I wasn't close to the shore so, I had to be cautious, and one mistake could end me up underwater. It was fun to jump with the waves. Soon, a huge wave came towards me. I tried to jump but my feet couldn't reach the bottom floor. I tried to swim up but it was too late because the water pushed me back the shore. "Wipeout!" My friends screamed.

I stood up and rushed to get my towel. As I ran, I accidently kicked sand onto a lady who was reading a book. "I am really sorry maam," I said. I then went to get my towel. I wiped up my face and arms and returned back into the water. Strangely, as I went back, I saw Evie, Ava, and Callie by the shore. They told me that a huge wave had crashed into them and pushed them off to shore. Callie had bruises all over her back. Evie and Ava had bruise marks on their legs. I felt pretty bad for them considering the fact that I didn't get any bruises when I had my wipe out. I waited for them to clean off their faces and we went back into the water.

Later on, we went to get some food to eat. There were sandwiches, chips, apples slices, carrot sticks, and water. I ate two sandwiches, some apples, chips, and carrots. When everyone was full, we went back into the water. We warmed up pretty good in the sun. But when we returned to the water, it was freezing. Since we were so cold, we left twenty minutes later. We headed to the bath house. I waited for my turn to take a bath. When it was my turn, I took my soap and shampoo and then stepped in. I took off my swimsuit, closed the curtain and started to get a wash. When I was ready to wash my hair, I couldn't find my shampoo.

I saw it floating under my stall and into the center place where things drained out. I didn't know what to do. "My shampoo floated away" I yelled out. Mrs. Kamil gave me another bottle so, I went back to my shower. Then I couldn't see my shoe. I looked under the stall and saw it the same place where the shampoo was. I tried to reach for it but it was too far away. I didn't know what to do so again. I then called Mrs. Kamil and told her that my shoe had floated away. She told me that she didn't know what to do. I got pretty worried because I couldn't walk around the boardwalk without a shoe. So I went on the floor and tried to get it. My hair had so much shampoo in it so when I went on the floor shampoo was everywhere. I still couldn't reach my shoe. My hair was all over my shoulders. And so was the shampoo so I rinsed it out and came out of the bathroom with one shoe on my foot. Evie asked me why I only had one shoe on. I told her what happened and she tried to help me get shoe. She told me that she couldn't reach it. I went into the dressing room, closed my curtain and put on my clothes. As I was dressing up I heard someone asking Evie and her mom what went wrong. They told her that my shoe was under the stall and in the center. The girl was wearing a swimsuit so she went under the stall, into the center and got my shoe out. People around cheered "Thank you!" "Natalie, someone got your shoe out of the stall" Evie said as I came out of my changing room. I was happy that my shoe was saved and that it wasn't lost.

When we left the bath house, we headed to the boardwalk. We went on a lot of rides like the Sea dragon, the Gravitron, and the Bumper Cars. After an hour and a half of fun, we went to get some ice cream. As we ate our ice cream we walked back to the beach. We sat in the sand and ate our ice cream. When we finished the last bite, we asked Mrs. Kamil for a beach ball. She handed Evie a deflated beach ball and she blew it up. Then we were ready to play.

It's a good thing that there were volleyball nets there. We threw the beach ball over the net back and forth but the wind kept blowing it away. Eventually, we stopped playing with the net. We threw the ball at each other then we gave the ball back to Mrs. Kamil and ran to the water. Since we had changed out of our swim clothes we couldn't go in the waters so we would wait to come near us and then we would run away from it. If the water touched us then the one that the water touched was out of the game until there is a winner. After thirty minutes we got all of our stuff and left.

On the way home, we made a stop at Grottos Pizza. We needed to make this stop so as to have something to eat at Evie's house when we reach there. We might get a late lunch if we didn't. We waited and waited and waited for our turn. Mrs. Kamil looked inside her purse and found a grottos pizza free ice cream sundae. She gave it to the lady at the front desk. She gave us our sundae with five spoons. The ice cream was chocolate with white whip cream and chocolate chips. Usually I don't eat chocolate ice cream but I made an exception since this one tasted awesome. After we ate our ice cream, the pizza was done. We grabbed the pizza and left the pizzeria.

Ten minutes later, we arrived at Evie's house. We went inside and sat down where the party was going to take place. I saw beef jerky, chips, chocolates, and pretzels. I saw four chairs at the table. I sat in one and so did everyone else. Evie's mom brought down the pizza. I got one slice of pepperoni, so did Ava. Callie and Evie got cheese pizza. We all said a blessing and ate our food. A few minutes later Mrs. Kamil came down stairs with Evie's birthday cake. It was an iCarly cake. We all sang happy birthday and ate the cake. When we finished, we ate some beef jerky and chips. The eating was done; we went to play a board game called Risk. As we played, Mrs. Kamil came downstairs and gave us iCarly rings that matched the birthday cake. Callie won the Risk. We all then went to bed.

During my sleep, I had a dream in which a dinosaur had grabbed me. Everyone tried to save me, and that got the dinosaur angry so then he spat out purple goo at them. The goo was so sticky that Evie stuck to the ground and couldn't get out. Then the monster ate me and there were dancing vegetables in his stomach. "There's a party in my tummy, so yummy, so yummy" they all sang. I danced and sang along until I woke up.

August 21, 2011
The Swimming Pool Miracle

"I am hungry," said auntie. She normally does not eat breakfast at the same time with us. She often ate much later after breakfast. Sometimes, lunch time is her breakfast time. "Oh! There are organic eggs in the refrigerator," I said. "I love organic eggs!" auntie continued. "You and my mom have many things in common!" I told her. My mom came home one day and told me that she found an organic store, that she was happy about her new discovery. "That is not good news for me because I know what was coming," I said. She laughed so hard. Later, without further notice, organic labels started to show up in our refrigerator.

School reopening was rapidly approaching. So, I focused on my readings most of the time. Any time this happened, I had to go in a separate area and stayed to myself to read. I felt bad for my cousins because, it seemed like they had lost a soul! They would remain quiet in their own quarters. They had no choice but to get their own books to help keep them busy to avoid being tempted to talking to me. Auntie had been helping them in their studies too. I took short breaks. During this time, I would either go to auntie or my cousins to stay with them for a little while.

I went to auntie and gave her my usual peck. Usually all the kids in the house often made their daily rounds. Sometimes, we would find ourselves in a single file just to get through our mealtime's-pecks routine. She cares a lot and pampers.

A conversation about swimming came up. She started to suggest a swimming outing and I mentioned a few places we could go to swim then, she remembered her past. Auntie told me that she couldn't swim in those days. She told me that she used to be like a rock that sunk in the water. But at least, she is better now. She told me a story about her experience in Nashville, Tennessee when she went swimming in the pool with my cousins.

Auntie Odiche went to a swimming pool with my the other of my cousins; Chi, Susan, Junior, and Maurine. Kathy was just a newborn this time. Chi and Susan had a floating device but auntie did not. "I went over to the 'deep' since I am tall enough to hold myself!" she assumed. Few moments later, she could not really hold herself up against the body of water any longer. She did not know how bad her swimming skills were. "I propped my head up above the water but it kept dropping, I was drowning!" she told me. Other adults were just comfortably seated around the area, very calm and chatting without paying attention to her. "I was gripped with fear," she said as she held her chest. "I struggled with that water, full-time! Water started to control me. It became increasingly difficult to be still." Then Chi and Susan came over. "Auntie Auntie Auntie!" they said in excitement, just expressing how they loved their swim. Auntie quickly seized them and this move helped to suspend her. She said she directed them so that all of them moved out of the pool. "That was my miracle" she said.

August 23, 2011
The Earthquake

My mom called me from work and had me give the phone to her sister, Auntie Odiche. I heard them giggling. I asked auntie the reason for that. She said that her friend, Brandy in Toronto called mom's cell phone by mistake. "Hi Odiche! Brandy!" Brandy said. "How can I help you?" mom answered. "Odiche, what happened to you? It is me Brandy?" Brandy replied. "But I do not know you? I am Odiche's sister, I am not Odiche," mom continued. Brandy quickly apologized and screamed in wonder. She said that she could not tell the difference between mom and auntie's voice.

Mom gave her the contact number for auntie and told her that auntie was at home. Mom was at work. She later called auntie to inform her about this. And they laughed and laughed. It was so funny.

We had our lunch and everybody scattered over the house doing one thing or the other. Mom had returned from work earlier today. I was just sitting down upstairs and noticed that the walls and my computer table were shaking. I paused to find out what was happening. My award certificate hanging on the wall then fell. I walked out of the room to ask my mom what happened. Earthquake earthquake! earthquake!" screamed my mom as she dived through the stairs in search for the other kids in the house. "Downstairs!" my auntie yelled out, waving her hand in a sweeping manner. I ran outside. "Come downstairs Natalie!" mom continued. I followed everyone. I was suddenly gripped with such a fear that made me want to crawl out of my skin! I then stopped and remembered we were not doing the right thing. "Mom, we need to stay outside because the building will cave into us." I headed outside as I shouted in fear. "You're right, upstairs. Outside everyone!" auntie shouted as she made her way towards outside through the front door. "Outside outside!" these words were forcefully coming out of my mom's mouth as she headed towards the door sweeping the kids along. Within two minutes, everyone was outside.

A neighbor opens the door. "It's earth quake! I do not know what to do!" she said in a terrified voice. Mom, auntie, me and all the rest of the kids held our hands and formed a circle outside and began to pray. The neighbor told us that it was the right thing to do.

Auntie then prayed

"Oh Lord! Send your hedge of protection over us. Release your power from your mighty throne in heaven to fight this battle for us for we are weak and weary. We have the assurance that you are already enthroned in our midst because your power is made perfect in our weakness. Let this earthquake not reach us. Let us behold your glory and live to the fullness of our years. We give you all the honor, glory and praise in Jesus name!" Everybody responded in one voice. Amen!

"What next!" my mom said. Auntie told everyone to sit down close together on the flower pavement outside. She started talking about Jesus and how he is the only one to help us out of the present situation.

"The earthquake seems to have stopped," auntie said slowly and quietly. "Let us all go inside and listen to the news." Mom then began to complain that she was lost and did not know that the earthquake was coming because the kids all watched their own programs in all the TVs in the house preventing the adults from listening to the news. We then tuned in to the local news and heard that the earthquake was felt throughout Washington DC, Boston, Virginia, Philadelphia, New Jersey and New York. "I want to go home" little Kathy cried out in her little voice. She curled herself around auntie and could hardly move. I have not seen her terrified before. She usually does most of the talking in her tiny but firm voice.

"I do not know what to do" I said in panic. "Jesus is what you do in a time like this" auntie said. "Remember that he is everything in time of danger! Pray in your mind now and talk to him." The other kids were just silent and listening. They were paralyzed with fear! Mom called dad and could not believe he was relaxed over the extremely horrifying earthquake incident. Mom was wondering the greatness of God and the amazing wonders of nature. "How could such a movement be felt so strongly, very huge and enormous over the entire east coastal regions of the United States." She said.

After the prayer, I noticed some peace inside me. This I told auntie and she was very pleased to hear this. As from then, I became very calm and had some strong feeling which made me feel safe.

Mom and auntie debated over picking up Sam from the day care. Auntie asked mom to think because she might be hurt on her way. She thought about it a little and then dashed into the car and headed towards the day care center. In about fifteen minutes she was back with Sam. She told auntie that the caregivers at the daycare advised to expect another even stronger hit by 4pm, an hour and half later. Auntie told everyone to wear their jeans and casual top precisely. We gathered few basic supplies, a tent and some food items which were loaded inside the car and mom drove everyone to a safe area where we stayed till at least, a quarter past four after which we returned home safely.

While we were away, I received a text from Evie. She told me that all that was to be expected was the aftershock wave which lessened by half every hour that passed by.

In the night, we all kept listening to the news for updates. We then heard this news that the aftershock would be happening within some days later. Also, hurricane Irene could affect those states close to the east coastline especially South Carolina and Virginia. I started to feel little convulsions inside me. "Hurricane Irene will not affect every inch of Delaware, every mile of Delaware even if it actually strikes. Okay? Everything is largely uncertain for now," explained auntie. "I am now relieved auntie," I said. We held our hands in a circle as usual and prayed over our safety.

August 24, 2011
Travelling Home

The touch of the earthquake stopped my happy summer experience cold. Today, mom had gone to work early. She called to inform us about the need to be updated on the news. "No other programs" she commanded. I handed auntie the phone per her request. "No more surprises!" she exclaimed. We then tuned in to the local news.

I told my auntie how my teacher explained the earthquake. My teacher said that everything that is hard could become soft in a second. The floor and roads, in a horrible earthquake, could start make wavy motions because of vibrations, school bus could be on the roof. Everything would seem unreal then. Talk of the earthquake had always been like a fairy tale. So, I thought I was dreaming but I pinched myself and would not wake up. Then I knew it was real!

Erin stepped in. "A long time ago probably, before our ancestors time. We did not have much earth quake and then the earth was new. But now that the earth is all rusty and old, the earthquake is happening to the old earth," he explained. "The last tornado we had, occurred last year and by then, we did not have a trampoline. We were so lucky because it did not hit our house, but it did hit the park and then the slide fell off. So we kind 'a glued the slide back. We kind 'a do not go to the slide anymore. We usually climbed to the top of the park. We climbed stunt bars and we now rather go on the swings. We do not go on the slides anymore because the tornado knocked it out and we glued it on. So, if we touched it we could break the slide and get hurt," Erin continued.

Hurricane Irene warning started to get more serious. The dear earthquake gave way into hurricane. "Now another lump in my throat," I panicked. It was all over the news. Kathy ran to auntie. "Hey auntie, are my family alright?"

Maurine told me that the hurricane had hit New York already," she panted. Why are you spreading false news?" auntie asked Maurine. "Hurricane Irene has only been predicted for the coming weekend, there is no incidence yet".

Mom tried to convince auntie not to travel over the weekend as they planned. Auntie called and knew that there were no cancellations, so the journey would continue.

Uncle Andrew called auntie and asked for my cousins to be brought back home to New York before it reached that area. They made an emergency preparation to leave either that night or the following morning. They then decided to leave in the early hours of the morning. I prepared a surprise pack for both Maurine and Kathy and handed it to them as they entered the taxi to be dropped off. Luckily they got there safely. They were welcomed and greeted by their parents and siblings. Auntie then made another emergency move to Toronto because New York was closing every business and public transportation system. We heard in the news "New York city, the city that never rests is going to sleep this time". Mom and auntie expected their husbands to return back from Nigeria within a space of a day, but were not sure since flights were being cancelled. So we prayed for safe and timely return of my dad and uncle Dede. Everything came through as expected.

Earthquake came through and no one was harmed
Hurricane came through and no one was harmed
Cousins and Auntie Odiche arrived New York City
on Saturday
Auntie arrived Toronto city on Sunday
Dad arrived Delaware on Sunday
Uncle Dede arrived Toronto city on Monday
So, it all went well
It all went well after all
I must say, I did enjoy my guests
My fun was the utmost
I could then say
It was a blissful summer!
And I must then say
Thank you my God !
THE END.

Ending remark

I will keep these memories in my keepsake,
they are the Pearl Drops in My Summer.
No ornament supersedes that woven with
precious stones dropping into my summertime.

Aunty Odiche and I